# FooTroT FlaTs 24

### By Murray Ball

ORIN BOOKS

PAGE FOUR

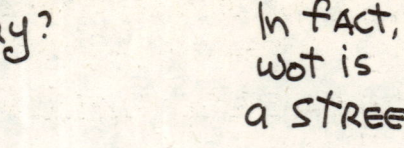

Just wot DO we no about Putiputi, enyway?

From a litter of Rangi Jones' Aunty Miriama wot ran off to Orkland to hav a good time eating Georgy pies (wot yew carnt get at Tokomaru Bay) and a bloke in a hood (Robin??)

May be! Becos Miriama & Robin wer REELY merry, man. But Puti cood not see wot they wer larfing at. The kichen wall was not that funny, eh?

So she went to live under a brij wot kept the cars off her hed but wot had trucks and that where there shood hav been WATER →

Then sumthing happened wot CHANGED her attitude compleetly...

"... LUV!"

Unbeleevably she discovered in the cuntry the RUFF, tuff, rip-rorin, roothless qualities wot she THORT ONLY lived in torn lether jackets in the big SITY...

The ULTIMATE TERMINATOR...

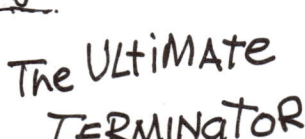

see back Page »→

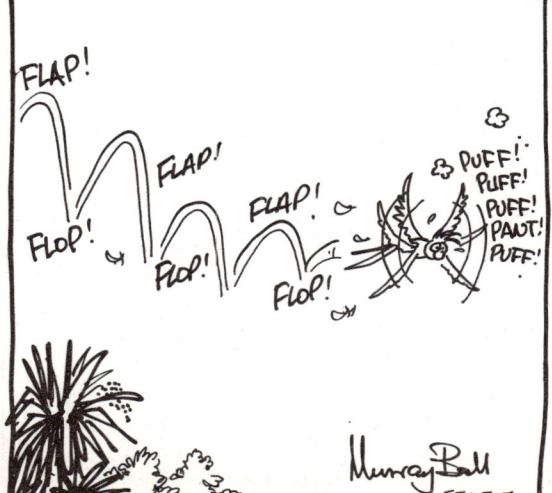

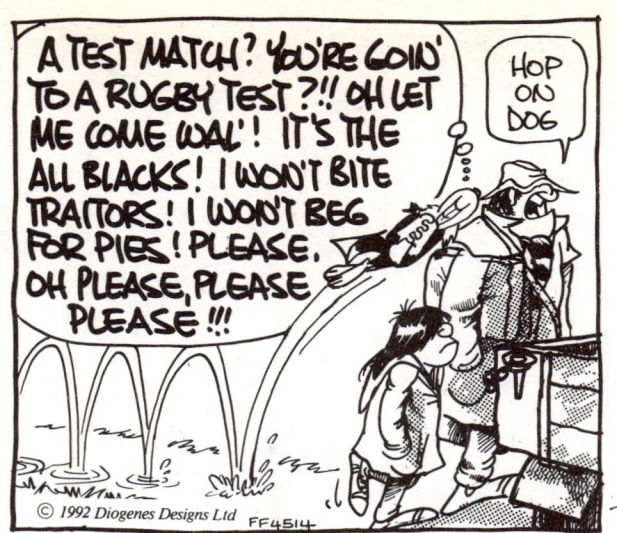

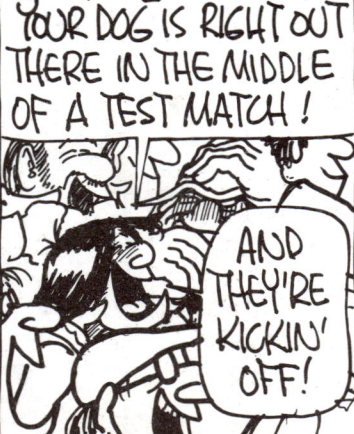

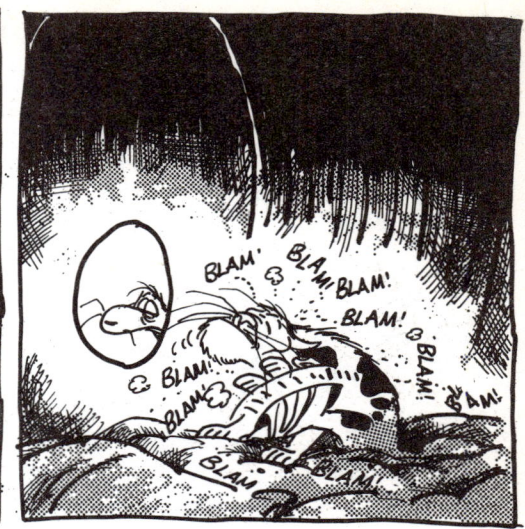

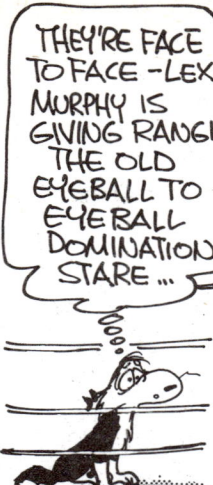

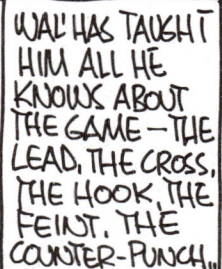

PAGE TWENTY NINE

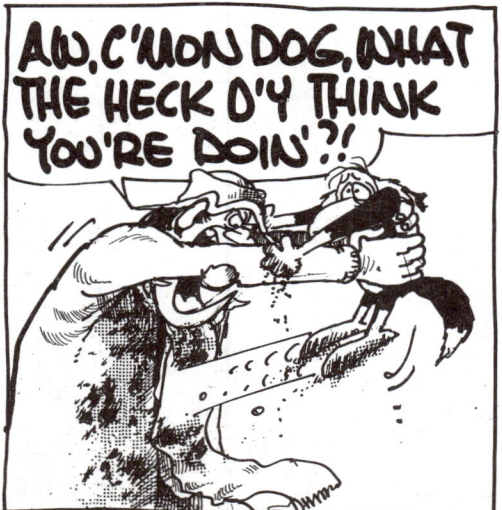

THE FEVER HAS DRIVEN CHEEKY HOBSON MAD - SHE THINKS I AM WAL', THE FOOL! I'M THE SLIM ONE!
© 1992 Diogenes Designs Ltd
LET ME GO YOU MAD WOMAN! I HAVE MY REPUTATION TO THINK OF!
ACTUALLY, IT'S NOT BAD IN HERE - SHE'S SORT OF SOFT AND WARM... I'LL COUNT TO TEN THEN RESUME THE STRUGGLE...
Z
PERVERT!!
SMAK!
Murray Ball
FF4565

WAL' IS IN THAT BEDROOM WITH CHEEKY HOBSON - I'VE GOT TO GET TO HIM...
Murray Ball
© 1992 Diogenes Designs Ltd
VRRROO-OOM!
FF4566
WHIRRRRRR... RRRR
SPRONG!
THIS IS NOT A HOUSE, IT'S A TORTURE CHAMBER!
WASHING LINE PEGS HERE
NOT HERE!

WHA'? IT'S THE MIDDLE OF THE NIGHT AND THERE IS SOMEONE IN CHEEKY HOBSON'S BEDROOM!
Murray Ball
© 1992 Diogenes Designs Ltd
WOOF! BOW RUFF!
WOOF! WOW RUFF!
WOOF! WOW RUFF!
WOOF! WOW! RUFF
WOOF! BOW RUFF
WOOF! WOW RUF
WOOF! WOW!
WOOF!
WOOF!
FF4567
GOD BLESS NEIGHBOURHOOD WATCH, EH, WAL'?

WELL, HERE WE ARE, ON OUR WAY HOME!
Murray Ball
CHEEKY HOBSON IS OVER HER FLU' AND WAL' IS OUT OF HER CLUTCHES...
...ONCE AGAIN (PUFF!) I FOILED THAT (PUFF) SCENTED SEDUCTRESS! (PUFF!) IT'S JUST ME AND (PUFF) WAL' AGAIN...
FF4568
BUDDIES! (PUFF! PUFF!) MATES! (PUFF!) PALS! (PUFF! PUFF! PUFF!)
ONE DAY (PUFF!) YOU'LL THANK ME (PUFF! PUFF!) FOR THIS!
© 1992 Diogenes Designs Ltd

I'M NOT LOOKIN' FORWARD TO THIS...
...FIRST TIME I'VE BEEN TO THE BACK OF THE FARM SINCE THE BIG STORM...
© 1992 Diogenes Designs Ltd
...I HATE TO THINK HOW MANY LAMBS AND KIDS WE WILL HAVE LOST... WHOOPS!
SCLOO-OOP!
FF 4569
WHIRRRR...RRRRRR...
Murray Ball.
WELL, I DIDN'T SEE TOO MANY PROBLEMS IN THAT PADDOCK...

ANOTHER LAMB THAT DIDN'T MAKE IT THROUGH LAST WEEKS STORM
© 1992 Diogenes Designs Ltd
...AND TWO MORE FOR THE DEAD LAMB SACK!
FF 4570
I FLAMIN' KNEW IT WOULD BE LIKE THIS!!
IF YOU FLAMIN' KNEW IT WOULD BE LIKE THIS WHY DIDN'T YOU BRING THE FLAMIN' HORSE TO CARRY THE FLAMIN' SACKS?!!
Murray Ball.

LOOK AT THAT– WE MUST HAVE LOST ALMOST HALF OUR NEW-BORN LAMBS AND KIDS IN LAST WEEK'S STORM!
IT MAKES YA FLAMIN' WONDER DOESN'T IT?
I MEAN, WHY DOES NATURE DO THIS SORT OF THING TO US?!!
WHY NOT?
© 1992 Diogenes Designs Ltd
FF4571

I HATE THE ENTRANCE TO THE COW YARD!
© 1992 Diogenes Designs Ltd
FF4572

WHAT'S YOUR PROBLEM, DOG? A BIT OF MUD AT THE COWSHED GATE WON'T HURT YOU!
AW, C'MON Y' BIG SOOK - IT'S NOT THAT BAD...
OKAY. MAYBE IT COULD DO WITH A BIT OF FILLER...
© 1992 Diogenes Designs Ltd
FF4573
Murray Ball

SPLOK!
GLUG! GLUG! GLUG! GLUG! GLUG! GLUG! GLUG! GLUG! GLUG! GLUG! GLUG!
GLUG! GLUG! GLUG! GLUG! GLUG! GLUG! GLUG! GLUG! GLUG! GLUG! GLUG! GLUG! GLUG!
CLONK!
SHUFFLE SHUFFLE
SHUFFLE SHUFFLE
SHUFFLE SHUFFLE
© 1992 Diogenes Designs Ltd
FF4574
Murray Ball

THE MUD IN THE COWYARD HAS GOT BEYOND A JOKE...
© 1992 Diogenes Designs Ltd
I'VE ORDERED A TRUCKLOAD OF GRAVEL TO FILL IT IN...
YEH, WELL IT'S A START
FF4575

ISN'T IT ALWAYS THE WAY?
... WE'VE HAD THE SLOPPY BOG-HOLE OF A COW YARD FILLED WITH GRAVEL SO IT IS NICE AND FIRM...
CHINK! CHINK! CLINK! CHONK!
© 1992 Diogenes Designs Ltd
NOW THE BLIMMIN' OLD COWS WON'T CROSS IT BECAUSE THEY DON'T LIKE THE FEEL OF IT!
FF4576

© 1992 Diogenes Designs Ltd
I SAID, 'I DON'T KNOW WHY YOU COME TO THE FARM IF YOU CAN'T STAND THE SILENCE!!'
FF 4577

IF YOU DON'T LIKE SILENCE WHY DO YOU COME TO THE COUNTRY ON HOLIDAY?!!
I SAID, ' IF YOU DON'T LIKE SILENCE...
CLICK!
HEY, SHUT YOUR FACE, MAN!!
FF 4578
...I CAN'T STAND YAPPIN' DOGS!
BOOT!
© 1992 Diogenes Designs Ltd

RANGI'S CHEEKY CITY COUSIN BOOTED ME OUT OF MY OWN WATERTANK TO USE IT AS A SOUND CAVERN FOR HER FLAMIN' GHETTO BLASTER!
Murray Ball
© 1992 Diogenes Designs Ltd
WELL, SHE TOOK ME BY SURPRISE, BUT I'M BACK! I'LL TELL HER WHAT I THINK OF HER BLIMMIN' MUSIC!
WHAM! BLAM BLAM! WHAM! BLAM BLAM BLAM
FF4579
GREAT ACOUSTICS

HAS IT OCCURRED TO YOU THAT IF YOU TURNED THE VOLUME DOWN YOU COULD HEAR THE WORDS?
WILL YOU SHUT UP THAT BARKIN'?!
I WAS MERELY OBSERVING THAT IF YOU TURNED DOWN THE VOLUME YOU MIGHT HEAR THE LYRICS...
© 1992 Diogenes Designs Ltd
FF4580
GOOD GRACIOUS!
...AND WE WILL...
WANNA DO IT...
...AND YOU CAN DO IT...
AND I WANT TO...
DON'T LISTEN!
Murray Ball.

WE'VE GOT TO GET THE OLD GIRL'S CALF OFF HER SO WE CAN TREAT ITS HORN BUDS...
FF4588
WHAM!!
MY JOB IS TO CREATE A DIVERSION...
© 1992 Diogenes Designs Ltd

IT IS MY JOB TO CREATE A DIVERSION TO ATTRACT THE MOTHER COW'S ATTENTION WHILE WAL' DEHORNS AND CASTRATES HER CALF...
FF4589
IT CAN BE A DANGEROUS BUSINESS
HERE SHE COMES...
WOOF WOOF! WOOF! WOOF!
YAP! YAP! YAP! YAP! YAP! YAP! YAP! YAP! YAP!
OH DEAR...
SORRY WAL'...
© 1992 Diogenes Designs Ltd

OKAY, NOW THIS SQUEEZE OF CAUSTIC SODA HAS GOT TO GO RIGHT ONTO THOSE HORN BUDS...
FF4590
...YOU'RE GONNA HAVE TO HOLD HIM VERY TIGHT...
AW HELLS BELLS I SAID 'HOLD TIGHT'!
CLUNK!
I AM HOLDING TIGHT!
© 1992 Diogenes Designs Ltd
Murray Ball

WELL THAT'S DONE, WE'VE PUT THE CAUSTIC SODA ON HIS HORN BUDS...
Murray Ball
FF 4591
...WE ALSO CLIPPED A PIECE OUT OF HIS EAR AND PUT A RUBBER RING ON HIS TESTICLES TO CASTRATE HIM.
NO HARD FEELINGS MATE...
© 1992 Diogenes Designs Ltd
C'MON. I DON'T BELIEVE IN HOLDING A GRUDGE!

SQUALL!
SNARL!
GRRRRRR
NAH, C'MON IT'S A COINCIDENCE!
Murray Ball
© 1992 Diogenes Designs Ltd
FF 4587

Murray Ball
FF4593
© 1992 Diogenes Designs Ltd
SIGH!

Murray Ball
FF4594
CREAK! RUMBLE! GURGLE!
© 1992 Diogenes Designs Ltd
CREAM OF CHICKEN SOUP AND CROÛTONS!

CREAK RUMBLE! GRUMBLE!
© 1992 Diogenes Designs Ltd
FF4595
IT'S NOT FAIR! THAT LITTLE SLOB HAD A HOT, PACKED LUNCH BUT WE DINKUM WORKIN' DOGS HAVE TO BATTLE FOR OURSELVES...
DON'T WORRY ABOUT ME, MATE. I'LL JUST GRAB A PASSING RABBIT!
WHO AM I KIDDING?
SNUFFLE SNUFFLE MUNCH CRUNCH...
SHOVE!
Murray Ball.

IT'S GETTING DARK—NOW WE'LL SEE WHO'S MADE OF THE RIGHT STUFF, MATE!
FF 4596
HAHA! CAN'T HACK IT, EH? GOIN' HOME TO MUMMY!
© 1992 Diogenes Designs Ltd
I DON'T BELIEVE IT— A PILLOW, WARM MILK AND A GINGERNUT!
DOES FLAMIN' AUNT DOLLY KNOW WHAT YOU'RE UP TO?!!
Murray Ball
Z
SHE THINKS HE'S ON AN OUTWARD BOUND SURVIVAL COURSE

HOWL!
FORGET IT, CHARLIE— BLUBBING NEVER GOT ANYONE ANYWHERE
FF 4597
HERE YOU ARE SWEETHEART— WAS THE LITTLE DARLING HUNGRY ON HIS BIG ADVENTURE?
© 1992 Diogenes Designs Ltd
HOOOWL!
WHAK!
Murray Ball.

FF4598
© 1992 Diogenes Designs Ltd
Z
LEAP!
JERK!

FF4599
© 1992 Diogenes Designs Ltd
AHEM!
Murray Ball

SMAK!
ACE!
FF 4600
SMAK!
ACE!
SMAK!
ACE!
I NEVER THOUGHT I'D SAY THIS - BUT I'LL BE QUITE GLAD WHEN CHEEKY HOBSON ARRIVES TO TAKE OVER...
© 1992 Diogenes Designs Ltd
Murray Ball.

SMAK!
FIFTEEN LOVE!
WHIRRR!
FF4601
SMAK!
THIRTY LOVE!
WHIRRR!
SMAK!
FORTY LOVE!
THOK!
WHIRR...
SPUT!
FIFTEEN FOR THE DOG
Murray Ball
© 1992 Diogenes Designs Ltd

THANK GOODNESS CHEEKY HOBSON HAS COME AT LAST
...IT'S PRETTY DARN BORING PLAYIN' TENNIS WHEN ONLY ONE BLOKE ON THE COURT CAN HOLD A RACKET
HERE Y'ARE DOG, YOU CAN PLAY WITH THESE OLD BALLS
ARE YOU KIDDING? THEY'RE COVERED WITH COLD DOG SPIT!
FF4602
© 1992 Diogenes Designs Ltd
Murray Ball

BORING! BORING! BORING!
Murray Ball.
FF4603
WOOF! YAP!
WOOF! YAP!
WOOF! YAP!
WOOF! YAP!
WOOF! YAP!
WOOF! YAP!
© 1992 Diogenes Designs Ltd
CLANG!
BALL BOY?

POK!
POK!
POK!
POK!
POK!
POK!
© 1992 Diogenes Designs Ltd
FF4604
GOOD BOY, THANK YOU
"GOOD" IS BETTER THAN "DEAD"
Murray Ball.

IN! POINT TO WAL'— WELL PLAYED WAL'!
CLAP! CLAP! CLAP! CLAP!
Murray Ball.
FF4605
OUT, DEFINITELY OUT! POINT TO WAL'! GOOD OLD WAL'!
OH, WELL PLAYED WAL'! GAME TO WAL'! HOORAY FOR WAL'! THREE CHEERS FOR...
CLUNK!
PENALTY GAME TO WAL'!!
© 1992 Diogenes Designs Ltd

HERE PIG, PIG...
SHAKE! SHAKE! SHAKE!
RATTLE! CLINK! CLANK! CLANG! RATTLE!
© 1992 Diogenes Designs Ltd
FF4606
WHUMP!
SQUEAL! SQUEAK! SQUEAL! SQUEAL!
OINK! OINK! OINK! OINK! OINK! OINK!
... PIG
Murray Ball

CLUNK!
WHOOPS!
© 1992 Diogenes Designs Ltd
FF4607
RUMBLE! RUMBLE! RUMBLE! RUMBLE: RUMBLE!
RUMBLE! RUMBLE! RUMBLE! RUMBLE!
WHUMP!
OINK! SQUEAK! SQUEAL! OINK!
THIS GIVES A WHOLE NEW MEANING TO THE TERM, "KICKING THE BUCKET"
Murray Ball.

CLINK!
CLUNK!
CLONK!
WHAM!
NO IT WAS NOT THE RATTLE OF YOUR BLASTED PIG-BUCKET!!
FF4608
© 1992 Diogenes Designs Ltd

HERE CHOOK, CHOOK, CHOOK!
RATTLE! RATTLE! RATTLE! RATTLE!
RUMBLE! RUMBLE! RUMBLE! RUMBLE!
WHAM!!!
IT'S NOT THE LYRICS, IT'S THE TUNE!
OINK! OINK! SQUEAL! SQUEAL!
GOBBLE! MUNCH CHOMP! GOBBLE!
FF4609
© 1992 Diogenes Designs Ltd

Murray Ball
FF4610
KRAK!
VRRROOM!
ANOTHER YEAR OLDER, ANOTHER YARD FASTER, WAL'...
© 1992 Diogenes Designs Ltd

RANGI CLEANED WAL' OUT WITH HIS FIRST BALL – WAL' IS GOIN' TO SHOW THE YOUNG BIG-HEAD HOW REAL CRICKETERS DO IT!
Murray Ball.
WHAK!
VRRR—OOOM!!
FF4611
© 1992 Diogenes Designs Ltd
NICE ONE, RANG'...

SWISH!
VRRR-OOM!
FF4612
Murray Ball
SWIPE!
VRRROOM!
© 1992 Diogenes Designs Ltd
SWISH!
SWIPE
SLASH!
AM I BOWLING TOO FAST, WAL'?
NO NO NO
YETH! YETH! YETH!

KRAK!
OOM!
FF4613
© 1992 Diogenes Designs Ltd
Murray Ball
VROOM! VROOM! VROOM! VROOM!
KRAK! KRAK! KRAK! KRAK!
VROOOM!
SMAK!
... SHOULDER AROUND AND STRETCH HIGHER WITH THAT DELIVERY ARM...

FF4614
© 1992 Diogenes Designs Ltd
SPRONG!
TOMATOES!
THE GREENHOUSE EFFECT!

FF4615
© 1992 Diogenes Designs Ltd
SAFE TANNING

THE EARTH IS HEATING UP...
...HUMAN BEINGS HAVE SO POLLUTED THE WORLD THAT THE ATMOSPHERE CAN'T HANDLE THEIR MUCK!
BY THIS TIME NEXT CENTURY WE COULD ALL BE FRYING!
STRETCH!
STILL, LOOK ON THE BRIGHT SIDE...
I'LL BE DEAD.
FF4616
© 1992 Diogenes Designs Ltd
Murray Ball.

POLLUTION IS CAUSING ATMOSPHERIC WARMING. TEMPERATURES ARE RISING EVERYWHERE
IT'S THE END OF THE WORLD, WE'RE GONNA FRY!
A REPRIEVE! A REPRIEVE!!
DUNNO. HE LIVES IN A WORLD OF HIS OWN...
FF4617
© 1992 Diogenes Designs Ltd
Murray Ball.

I HATE THEM, THE WHOLE HUMAN RACE!
LOOK WHAT THEY'VE DONE TO THE WORLD — DESTROYED THE OZONE LAYER AND PUT SO MUCH FILTH INTO THE ATMOSPHERE WE'RE ALL GOIN' TO FRY!!
YOU FILTHY, CORRUPT, MATERIALISTIC SONS OF ADAM ARE A DISGRACE TO THE ANIMAL KINGDOM!!!
THE SWINE!!!
TEA TIME
FF4620
© 1992 Diogenes Designs Ltd

G'DAY IRISH, WHAT ARE Y' UP TO?
FIXIN' OUR RABBIT PROBLEM ONCE AND FOR ALL...
...WE'RE GONNA RELEASE SOME RABBIT FLEAS CARRYIN' MYXOMATOSIS!
OVER MY DEAD BODY!
© 1992 Diogenes Designs Ltd
FF4630

I'VE GOT A PROBLEM WAL'...
...THE MURPHYS WERE RELEASIN' MYXOMATOSIS FLEAS - I HAD A BIT OF A SCUFFLE WITH THEM AND I'VE BEEN COLONISED - THEY'RE DRIVIN' ME NUTS!
FF4631
A MAN CAN'T LET HIS BEST MATE CARRY THE CAN FOR DOIN' WHAT'S RIGHT — I'LL SEEYA RIGHT, MATE
GREATER LOVE HATH NO MAN, WAL'...
RUB! RUB! RUB! RUB!
© 1992 Diogenes Designs Ltd

DON'T WORRY DOG— WOULD I LEAVE YOU COVERED IN FLEAS?
YOU MIGHT
FF4632
...I'LL JUST GET THE FLEA POWDER AND... OH DEAR... IT'S EMPTY. SORRY DOG!
LOOK, JUST FIND A COMFY PLACE OUT OF THE SUN AND I'LL GET SOME MORE POWDER WHEN I GO TO TOWN... RIGHT?
RIGHT!
© 1992 Diogenes Designs Ltd

UNCLE WAL', I'VE CHANGED MY MIND!..
...I'M NOT BORED ANY MORE...
FF4624
© 1992 Diogenes Designs Ltd

© 1992 Diogenes Designs Ltd
CHOP!
FF4625
I NEED MY WALKMAN

HACK! HACK! HACK! HACK!
MAN, IT'S HOT!
HERE Y'ARE DOG, LOOK AFTER MY WALKMAN FOR A WHILE!
GOOD GRACIOUS!!
WHO D'Y THINK YOU'RE YELLIN' AT?!!
FF4626
© 1992 Diogenes Designs Ltd

THEY SAY MUSIC CROSSES ALL LANGUAGE BARRIERS...
CLIK! CLIK! CLIK!
WE ALL SPEAK HARLEM, MAN!
© 1992 Diogenes Designs Ltd
FF4627

GOOD GRACIOUS!
© 1992 Diogenes Designs Ltd
OH DEAR...
FF4628
OH DEAR OH DEAR OH DEAR
SEX AND SUBSTANCE ABUSE HAS MADE THEM MAD!

DA DA DADA DA DA DOOP...
© 1992 Diogenes Designs Ltd
DA DA DOOP DA
ZWOT!
FF4629
DADA D.DA
ZWOT!
DOOPA DOOP DAD...
ZWOT!
ZWAK
ZWAK!
BLASTED ELECTRIC FENCE!

AW, STOP Y' BELLY-ACHIN'! HE'S ONLY WATCHIN'!
© 1992 Diogenes Designs Ltd
FF4633
Murray Ball.

... FORTY - LOVE
VRRR-RROOM
© 1992 Diogenes Designs Ltd
... GAME, SET AND MATCH TO NIGEL ERSKINE
FFIZZZZZZ...
FF4634
WALLACE!
KRICKLE! KRAK KRAK CRUNCH

PAGE SIXTY SIX

C'MON CHEEKY, Y' CAN'T GO TO THE CLUB BALL WITH THAT BURK, ERSKINE!
I CAN AND I WILL, ESPECIALLY AFTER THAT FEARFUL BLOW YOU STRUCK HIM!
Murray Ball
...IT WAS ONLY A TAP WITH A RACQUET...
LOOK, YOU CAN'T GO!!
AND WHY NOT?
BECAUSE...
BECAUSE I LOVE Y...
HOIK!
© 1992 Diogenes Designs Ltd
COME, COME WALLY, I'M SURE CHEEKY ISN'T INTERESTED IN HOW YOU FEEL ABOUT ME...
FF4637

I'M WORRIED ABOUT WAL'. I KNOW HE'S UPSET ABOUT CHEEKY HOBSON GOIN' TO THE TENNIS CLUB BALL WITH THAT SLEAZY BUT VIRILE NIGEL ERSKINE!
© 1992 Diogenes Designs Ltd
WAL' DOESN'T GO TO BALLS AND I'M WORRIED THAT IN THIS HIGHLY EMOTIONAL STATE HE MIGHT DO SOMETHING FOOLISH...
CLICK!
FF4638
Murray Ball

CLUB ROOMS
WELL, HERE WE ARE AT THE TENNIS CLUB BALL— IN YA GO WAL'...
Murray Ball
© 1992 Diogenes Designs Ltd
WELL? GO ON! GO ON, WHAT ARE Y' WAITING FOR? I DARE YA! I DOUBLE DARE YA!!
FF 4639
HEH HEH! I KNEW HE'D CHICKEN OUT. I KNOW MY MAN.
ARE YOU MAD?!!
THWOK!

WAL', YOU'VE COME TO THE BALL!
YOU NEVER COME TO BALLS
© 1992 Diogenes Designs Ltd
I CAN'T THINK WHY YOU CAME THIS TIME — LOOKING SO DASHING TOO, IN WHITE TIE, TOP HAT
FF 4640
TENNIS CLUB
...AND TAIL!
Murray Ball

WILL OUR GUESTS OF HONOUR, DAHLENE AND NIGEL PLEASE LEAD OFF THE DANCING...?
WHAT'S UP FOOTROT. NO ONE TO DANCE WITH?
SIGH
© 1992 Diogenes Designs Ltd
FF4641
Murray Ball

WHAT A FOOL I WAS TO COME TO THIS BALL!
I BLEW IT WITH CHEEKY-BOY, DID I LOOK A WALLY!!
... 'COURSE, THIS IS THE CLASSIC MOVIE SCENE ... BOY BOWED AND DEFEATED HAS LOST THE GIRL...
...BECOMES AWARE OF A SILENT PRESENCE– THE FRAGRANCE OF A WELL-REMEMBERED PERFUME... A SOFT TOUCH ON HIS SHOULDER..!!
© 1992 Diogenes Designs Ltd
FF4643
Murray Ball

Murray Ball
PLEASE GOD, GIVE US RAIN.
FF4648
HE SAID "NO"
© 1992 Diogenes Designs Ltd

FF4649
© 1992 Diogenes Designs Ltd
IS THIS YOUR IDEA OF A JOKE?!!
Murray Ball.

C'MON GOD, YOUR LAND IS BURNING! YOUR PLANTS ARE DYIN'! YOUR ANIMALS ARE SUFFERING! C'MON, PLEASE GIVE THEM SOME RAIN!
IT'S NO GOOD. I JUST CAN'T STOP THAT LITTLE TOUCH OF SELF-INTEREST CREEPIN' IN...
© 1992 Diogenes Designs Ltd
Murray Ball
FF 4650

WAL' LOOK IT'S RAINING! THE DROUGHT HAS BROKEN!
IT'S NOT GONNA RAIN, IS IT GOD? YOU'RE JUST PULLIN' MY LEG TO TORMENT ME.
WELL I'M NOT FOOLED, I'VE SEEN IT BEFORE! Y'CAN'T HURT ME ANY MORE!
WAAAGH!!
Murray Ball
© 1992 Diogenes Designs Ltd
FF 4651

CRIPES COOCHIE, WHAT A SUMMER, EH?
...THE DAMS ARE EMPTY, SOIL IS CRACKIN', LEAVES CURLIN' ON THE TREES AND THE SUN RAISES BLISTERS – IT'S LIKE THE CLIMATE HAS GOT IT IN FOR US AND IS TRYIN' TO BLOW US AWAY...
C'MON CLIMATE WHAT HAVE WE EVER DONE TO YOU?!!
DON'T ASK
GREENHOUSE EFFECT
NOT PROVEN
OZONE LAYER
NO PROBLEM
© 1992 Diogenes Designs Ltd
FF4674

WELL I DON'T FEEL GUILTY!
I DON'T BELIEVE OUR POLLUTION HAS CAUSED A GREENHOUSE EFFECT! I RECKON IT IS JUST A NATURAL SPELL OF WARM WEATHER!
WHAT HAVE WE DONE?
FF4676
© 1992 Diogenes Designs Ltd

UNCLE WAL', WHAT'S THE SARGASSO SEA?
© 1992 Diogenes Designs Ltd
... PART OF THE ATLANTIC OCEAN—FULL OF WEEDS AND OLD WRECKS...
...LIKE THE FRONT LAWN?
Murray Ball
FF 4664

LOOK WHAT IS MOST IMPORTANT...?
...FENCIN' THE TOP PADDOCK, DRENCHIN' THE EWES, SPRAYIN' THE BLACKBERRY, DOSIN' THE COWS, FIXIN' THE SHORT IN THE ELECTRIC FENCE, REPAIRIN' THE FLOODGATE OR KILLIN' THE ROOSTERS?!!
FF 4665
ALL RIGHT! ALL RIGHT! ALL RIGHT!
...I'LL MOW THE BLOODY LAWN!!
Murray Ball
© 1992 Diogenes Designs Ltd

Murray Ball.
FF4657
RUB! RUB! RUB! RUB!
ONE LIKES TO BE IN THE GAME.
© 1992 Diogenes Designs Ltd

THE THING I LIKE ABOUT CRICKET IS IT IS MORE A 'FUN' GAME... NO WIN-AT-ALL-COSTS, NO HEROICS...
© 1992 Diogenes Designs Ltd
FF4658
CRAK!!
CATCHIT DOG!!
WHIRRR RRR...
HEH HEH, SIX!
VRRROOO OOM!
Murray Ball.

I MISSED A CATCH OFF WAL'S BOWLING. I'VE BEEN BANISHED TO THE DEEP, LONG-ON BOUNDARY...
Murray Ball.
FF4659
I RESENT THIS! NOBODY COULD HAVE CAUGHT THAT BALL, IT WAS GOIN' LIKE A BULLET!!
© 1992 Diogenes Designs Ltd
WHIRRR... RRRR
SMAK!
YEH, BUT IN YOUR TEETH, IN YOUR TEETH!!

AT LAST! MY BIG CHANCE! WAL' HAS SELECTED ME TO FIELD IN THE SLIPS!
Murray Ball
FF4660
SLIP FIELDERS CAN WIN OR LOSE A GAME! THEY MUST BE EAGLE-EYED AND EVER ALERT...
...THEY MAY HAVE TO WAIT FOR HOURS AND HOURS FOR THAT VITAL CATCH THAT COULD WIN OR LOSE THE GAME...
SNIK!
© 1992 Diogenes Designs Ltd
C'MON WAL', IT'S ONLY A GAME!!
RUMBLE! RUMBLE! RUMBLE! RUMBLE! RU

Murray Ball
FF4652
© 1992 Diogenes Designs Ltd
WAL' WE'VE GOT GOATS IN THE BUSH!!

PEOPLE HAVE LET THEIR ELECTRIC FENCES FALL INTO DISREPAIR SINCE THE PRICE OF GOATS HAS FALLEN...
...HERDS OF FERAL GOATS ARE ROAMIN' THE COUNTRY RAVISHIN' OUR BUSH.
© 1992 Diogenes Designs Ltd
THEY'RE GONNA HAVE TO BE WIPED OUT- WE'RE GONNA HAVE TO EXTERMINATE THEM BEFORE THEY DESTROY EVERYTHING...
THEN WE'LL HAVE TO DEAL WITH THE GOATS.
FF4653

Panel 1: "I DON'T WANT TO JUMP TO CONCLUSIONS— MAYBE IT WASN'T GOATS WHO KILLED THIS BUSH..."

Panel 2: "...MAYBE IT WAS A NATURAL DISASTER—MAYBE WE'VE GOT NO GOAT PROBLEM..."

Panel 4: "NOPE, WE'VE GOT A PROBLEM."

Panel 5: "FOR CRYIN' OUT LOUD, GOATS, STOP THIS DESTRUCTION!"

Panel 6: "...IF YOU KEEP EATING THE LEAVES AND BARK THE TREES WILL ALL DIE!"

Panel 7: "WELL, YOU MAY SAY THAT—"

Panel 8: "...BUT I'M AFRAID 'IT'S THEM OR US' IS ONLY A VALID ARGUMENT WHEN USED BY HUMAN BEINGS."

BELIEVE ME, I'VE GOT NOTHING AGAINST GOATS AS SUCH - IT'S JUST THAT WHERE YOU HAVE A POPULATION PROBLEM...
WHIRRR...RRRR
RATTLE! RATTLE! RATTL RATT
CHINK! CLINK! CHINK! CLINK! RATTLE CLINK!
... YOU HAVE A WASTE DISPOSAL PROBLEM...
© 1992 Diogenes Designs Ltd

HEH HEH, AUNT DOLLY IS TRYIN' TO RUN OFF HER CHRISTMAS FAT...
Murray Ball
THEY ALL TEND TO OVER DO IT AT THIS TIME OF YEAR...
... FORTUNATELY WE DOGS SHOW A LITTLE MORE INNER STRENGTH WHEN IT COMES TO DIET...
FF4667
© 1992 Diogenes Designs Ltd
AW CRIPES WAL'!!
PLUM PUDDING, CUSTARD, TRIFLE AND CHRISTMAS CAKE WITH MARZIPAN ICING?!!

CURSE MY CHRISTMAS FAT!
RIGHTO, NOTHIN' BUT DRY BISCUITS AND WATER FOR A WEEK!
Murray Ball
FF4671
PHEE-EEP!!
OI, DOG!
COOCH
LOOK WHAT I SAVED FOR YOU—HAPPY CHRISTMAS, MATE!
© 1992 Diogenes Designs Ltd
OH COOCHIE, PAVLOVA AND TRIFLE... HOW LOVELY

AEROBICS
THEY RECKON GOIN' TO AEROBICS IS A GOOD WAY TO GET RID OF CHRISTMAS FAT...
© 1992 Diogenes Designs Ltd
Murray Ball
FF4672
EVERYBODY READY? RIGHT, HIT IT!!
...AND RELAX!
CLAP! CLAP! CLAP! CLAP!
CLAP! CLAP! CLAP! CLAP!
I HOPE IT WORKS

> We luv each other! We AR movin in together!

She is a dum kid! On the uther hand, Wal' shood BE so dum! Wen it cums to choosin a partner for LIFE Cheeky Hobson makes a CHAINSORE look GOOD!!!

See ya in Book 25!

Luve
(Sum say 'luv' has a 'e'. Dus not look rite, eh?)
The Dog —
xxx